T0071048

Wenceslas

Bob Chilcott

for mezzo-soprano and baritone soloists, SATB chorus, and piano or orchestra

Vocal score

MUSIC DEPARTMENT

OXFORD
UNIVERSITY PRESS

OXFORD
UNIVERSITY PRESS

Great Clarendon Street, Oxford OX2 6DP,
United Kingdom

Oxford University Press is a department of the University of Oxford.
It furthers the University's objective of excellence in research, scholarship,
and education by publishing worldwide. Oxford is a registered trade mark of
Oxford University Press in the UK and in certain other countries

© Oxford University Press 2014

Bob Chilcott has asserted his right under the Copyright, Designs
and Patents Act, 1988, to be identified as the Composer of this Work

First published 2014

Impression: 4

All rights reserved. No part of this publication may be reproduced,
stored in a retrieval system, or transmitted, in any form or by any means,
without the prior permission in writing of Oxford University Press

Permission to perform this work in public (except in the course of divine worship)
should normally be obtained from a local performing right licensing organization,
unless the owner or the occupier of the premises being used already holds
a licence from such an organization. Likewise, permission to make and
exploit a recording of these works should be obtained from a
local mechanical copyright licensing organization

Enquiries concerning reproduction outside the scope of the above
should be directed to the Music Rights Department, Oxford University Press,
at music.permissions.uk@oup.com or at the address above

ISBN 978-0-19-340476-2

Music origination by Enigma Music Production Services, Amersham, Bucks.
Printed in Great Britain on acid-free paper by
Halstan & Co. Ltd, Amersham, Bucks.

Contents

Composer's note 4

1. Wintertide (chorus) 5
2. Who can that be? (Page, Wenceslas, and chorus) 15
3. Forth they went (Page, Wenceslas, and chorus) 21
4. Interlude — Winter Dark (piano or orchestra) 27
5. Sleeping in winter's arms (Page, Wenceslas, and chorus) 30
6. Thank you (Page and chorus) 39
7. Fanfare — Winter Bright (piano or orchestra) 44
8. On Saint Stephen's Night (Wenceslas, chorus, and audience or semi-chorus) 46

Composer's note

Written for the 150th anniversary of the iconic John Lewis store in Oxford Street, London, *Wenceslas* recalls through the poetic text by Charles Bennett the tenth-century Czech legend of a good king and his page. These two characters, here taking the form of baritone and mezzo-soprano soloists, brave the winter weather on St Stephen's Night to give a poor man shelter. The piece is through-composed, but movements 4 and 7, originally written as orchestral interludes, can be omitted if the piece is performed with piano accompaniment. Similarly, wide chords in the piano part may be spread where necessary.

Wenceslas makes use of the well-known carol 'Good King Wenceslas', spreading the five verses of text by J. M. Neale (1818–66) over several movements, and the melody 'Tempus adest floridum' (from *Piae Cantiones* 1582) appears in both original and altered forms.

Duration: *c.*24 minutes

An accompaniment for orchestra (2 fl, 2 ob, 2 cl, 2 bsn, 2 hn, 2 tpt, timp, 2 perc, hp, str) is available on hire/rental from the publisher or appropriate agent.

Commissioned by John Lewis to celebrate the 150th anniversary of the founding of the business in 1864, for first performance at the Royal Albert Hall on 1 December 2014, performed by the John Lewis Partnership's own choirs and orchestra, conducted by Manvinder Rattan.

Choirs of the John Lewis Partnership Music Society:

Voices in Partnership
The Cavendish Singers
The Lunchtime Choir
A Choired Taste
Cambridge Capella
Auld Reekie
Côr Alaw'r Fenai
Tartan Tones
Croydon Counterpoint
Junction 4
Thames Valley Voices

with

The Cavendish Ensemble

Wenceslas

Charles Bennett (b. 1954)

BOB CHILCOTT

1. Wintertide

Music © Oxford University Press 2014. Text © Charles Bennett. Reproduced by permission of the author.

Printed in Great Britain

OXFORD UNIVERSITY PRESS, MUSIC DEPARTMENT, GREAT CLARENDON STREET, OXFORD OX2 6DP

The Moral Rights of the Composer have been asserted. Photocopying this copyright material is ILLEGAL.

12
15
18
dim.
mf
21
dim.
LH
p
25

28
S.
A.
T.
B.
p
sfp
f
Lis - ten to the storm!
When snow's this deep it's good to sleep and
31
warm.
keep your - self warm, keep your - self warm.
Lis - ten to the
34
storm!
When snow's this deep it's good to sleep and keep your - self warm,
warm.

37
mf
keep your-self warm.
A - no - ther drink.
Don't think of
mf
Have a - no - ther drink.
Don't e - ven think of
mf
40
f
go - ing out-side.
mf
Frost and moon
sing a win - ter tune,
so
f
go - ing out - side.
mf
Frost and moon sing a tune,
so
f
mf
43
f
stay by my side, my side.
p
f
p
f

46
p
Pi - ty a - ny poor soul out in the cold,
pp
Good King Wen - ces - las looked out
p
50
frost for a blan - ket, ice in their bones.
On the feast of Ste - phen,
53
Pi - ty for the wretch who sleeps out - side by them - selves at
When the snow lay round a - bout, Deep, and crisp, and

56
win - ter - tide.
e - ven.
60
p
sfp
f
Stay by my side,
stay by my side at
win - ter - tide.
63
p
sfp
win - ter - tide,
win - ter-tide.
Stay by my side,

67
f
win - ter - tide.
stay by my side at win - ter - tide, win - ter - tide.
f
f
70
mf
f
Warm as toast, we're sa - tis - fied.
mf
f
Warm as toast, as chest-nuts roast, we're sa - tis - fied.
mf
f
73
mf
f
Let's hi - ber - nate till a lat - er date, so close your eyes, your
mf
Let's hi - ber - nate, so
f
mf
f

76
p
eyes.
p
p
80
p
Pi - ty a - ny poor soul out in the cold, frost for a blan - ket, ice in their bones.
pp
Bright - ly shone the moon that night, Though the frost was cru - el,
84
Pi - ty for the wretch who sleeps out - side by them-selves at
When a poor man came in sight, Ga - th'ring win - ter

88
win - ter - tide.
fu - - el.
92
p
mp
Close your eyes. Frost and moon sing a win - ter tune, it's cold out - side.
96
keep our - selves warm.
Have a - no - ther drink. Let's not think, just keep our - selves warm. When

100
mp dolce
sleep.
Lis - ten to the
snow's this deep it's good to sleep, to sleep.
Lis - ten to the
sleep, sleep.
mp dolce
good to sleep, to sleep.
mp dolce
104
storm!
Lis - ten to the storm!
dim.
storm, the storm!
Lis - ten to the storm, the
dim.
107
p
storm!
Lis - ten to the storm!
p
p
pp

2. Who can that be?

13
mp
PAGE
me.
From the cut of his cloth,
un-der the hill by St Ag-nes'
mp
17
mf espress.
well.
From hand to mouth he lives as he may from day to day, a
mf espress.
21
league or two south, a league or two south.
mp
25
WENCESLAS mp
Come with me, we'll take him cheer this time of year and

29
mf espress.
see if we can make things bright on Ste-phen's Night for cha - ri - ty, for
mf espress.
33
cha - ri - ty.
mp
mf
38
PAGE
mp
mf
PAGE
There's a man in the snow, a man in the snow with
WENCESLAS
mp
mf
WEN.
There's a man in the snow with
T./B. unis.
p
T./B.
'Hi - ther, page, and stand by me, If
mp
mf

42
no-where to go. Come with me, come with me.
no-where to go. Come with me, come
thou know'st it, tell - ing, Yon - der pea -
46
PAGE
The man in the snow, he's fa - mi - liar to me.
WEN.
with me.
mp
Come with
S./A.
S./A. unis. p
'Sire, he lives
T./B.
- sant, who is he? Where and what his dwell - ing?'
mp

50
mf
VEN.
me, come with me un-der the hill by Saint Ag-nes' well. We'll
S./A.
a good league hence, Un - der - neath the moun - tain, Right
T./B.
54
PAGE mf espress.
PAGE
We'll take him cheer this time of year for
VEN.
take him cheer; we'll take him cheer at this time of year for cha - ri - ty,
S./A.
a - gainst the fo - rest fence, By Saint Ag - nes' foun -
T./B.
mf espress.

58
cha - ri - ty, for cha - ri -
cha - ri - ty, for cha - ri -
- - tain.'
63
mp
- ty, cha - ri - ty.
mp
- ty, for cha - ri - ty.
rit.
p
p
p
pp
Cha - ri - ty.
p
pp
rit.
mp
p
attacca

3. Forth they went

13
S.
mp
A.
We'll take him shoes so wa - ter - tight to
mp
17
wrap his feet a-gainst the night.
21
WENCESLAS
f
WEN.
Bring me flesh, and bring me wine, Bring me pine - logs
S.
A.
mf
We'll take a loaf so good and fresh to feed the soul and feed the
T.
B.
mf
mf

25
hi - ther: Thou and I will see him dine,
flesh. We'll take him tin - der and a spark to
29
When we bear them thi - ther.
make a blaze a - gainst the dark. We'll
f
f

32
PAGE
f
PAGE
Page and mo - narch, forth they went, Forth they went to -
WEN.
Page and mo - narch, forth they went, Forth they went to -
S.
A.
take him laugh - ter in a jest, to ease his heart and bring him
T.
B.
f
35
- ge - ther: Through the rude wind's wild la - ment
- ge - ther: Through the rude wind's wild la - ment
rest. We'll take him warmth and show we care, Saint

38
ff
And the bit - ter wea - - ther.
And the bit - ter wea - - ther.
Ste-phen's Night shall last all year, all year, all
42
dim.
S.
A.
year, all year, all
T.
B.
dim.

46
f dim.
mf
year, all year.
f dim.
mf
f dim.
mf
51
S./A. umis. mp
Saint
mp
56
Ste-phen's Night shall last all year,
Saint Ste-phen's Night shall last all year,
T./B. unis. mp
Saint Ste-phen's Night shall last all year,
Saint Ste-phen's Night shall last all

4. Interlude — Winter Dark

6
poco rit.
a tempo
p
mf
11
p
15
cresc.
poco rit.
f
a bit slower
mp
20
a tempo
p
24
3
mp
poco rit.
29
a tempo poco tenuto
p

34
mf
39
f
45
mf dim.
poco rit.
p
50
a tempo
mf
54
p
mf
poco rit.
f
59
a bit slower
rit.
pp
attacca

5. Sleeping in winter's arms

13
f
How much fur - ther can it be? One more step.
f
f
17
Snow will be the death of me. Near - ly there yet?
21
ff
When all's said and done and i - ci - cles
ff
ff

25
come to freeze my tongue with win - ter's song,
30
mf
I'll be dead and gone, come to harm, sleep - ing in
mf
mf
35
f
win - ter's arms.
f
f

40
PAGE
PAGE mp
Sire, the night is
S.
A.
mf dim.
mp
45
dark - er now,
And the wind blows strong - er;
is dark - er now,
S. pp
A. p
is dark - er now,
50
Fails my heart, I know not how;
strong - er.
pp
p
strong - er.
p
I
pp
I know not how,

55
I can go no long - er.
know not how,
no long - er.
pp
p
no long - er.
WENCESLAS
60
f
Mark my foot - steps, good my page; Tread thou in them bold - ly:
f
65
Thou shalt find the win - ter's rage Freeze thy blood less cold - ly.

71
S.
A.
T.
B.
mf
If I should fall a - mongst the snow, say that
mf
mf
76
I was just a fro - zen spar - row, too cold to fly. If
81
f
I should die be - fore I wake, wrong or right, I pray the Lord my
f
f

86
soul to take and say good - night. When
90
PAGE
ff
PAGE
Sire, the night is dark - er now, And the
WENCESLAS
ff
WEN.
Mark my foot - steps, good my page; Tread thou in them
ff
S.
A.
all's said and done and i - ci - cles come to freeze my
T.
B.
ff
ff

95
wind blows strong - er; Fails my heart, I
bold - ly: Thou shalt find the win - ter's rage
tongue with win - ter's song, I'll be dead and gone,
100
know not how; I can go no long - er.
Freeze thy blood less cold - - - ly.
come to harm, sleep - ing in win - ter's arms,

106
S.
A.
mf
sleep - ing in win - ter's
T.
B.
mf
mf
110
mp
rit.
arms,
mp
rit.
mp
Slow ♩ = c. 58
114
p
sleep - ing in win - ter's arms.
p
Slow ♩ = c. 58
p
p
attacca

6. Thank you

Ballad style ♩ = c.88
PAGE
SOPRANO
ALTO
TENOR
BASS
Ballad style ♩ = c.88
p sost.
con Ped.
5
PAGE p
1. Ne-ver thought I'd make it this far, Bless my luck - y star.
2. Ne-ver thought I'd find the time to give you all that's mine.
9
Did-n't think I could feel a - ny-thing this real.
Did-n't think I'd lose my fear. You made it dis - ap - pear.

13
Ne-ver thought I'd find my-self here at the end of a-no - ther year.
Ne-ver thought we'd come that close. It hap-pens, I sup-pose.
17
Did-n't think that this could come true. Thank you, thank you.
Did-n't think I'd lose my fear. You made it dis-ap-pear.
For what-
21
mf
PAGE
- ev- er you've been told, young or old, it's time to come in from the cold.
For what-
S.
mp
Young or old,
A.
mp
div.
oo
oo
T.
B.
mp
oo
oo
mf

25
- ev-er you've been told, young or old, it's time to come in from the cold,
young or old.
unis.
oo
oo
29
1.
2.
p
mf
AGE
in from the cold.
in from the cold.
S.
A.
mf
In from the cold.
T.
B.
mf
1.
2.
p

31
mf
S.
A.
Ne-ver thought I'd touch the sky. How sur-prised am I?
T.
B.
mf
mf
35
f
Did-n't think that dreams come true. Thank you, thank you.
f
f
39
p
p
p sost.

44
PAGE
p
PAGE
Ne-ver thought I'd find my-self here at the end of a-no - ther year.
S.
A.
T.
B.
48
rit.
Did-n't think that this could come true.
Thank you, thank you, thank you.
p
oo
Thank you, thank you.
p
rit.
attacca

7. *Fanfare — Winter Bright*

28
mf
33
f
39
44
50
mf
f
56
ff
attacca

8. On Saint Stephen's Night

14
S.
A.
T.
B.
mp dolce
mf
A log on the fire was a tree in the fo - rest,
mp dolce
mf
mf
18
mp
A tree in the fo - rest, who grew so high.
mp
mp
22
mf ma dolce
burn - ing,
Now be - neath his roof it's burn - ing, it's burn - ing,
mf ma dolce
burn - -
mf ma dolce

26
burn - ing, burn - ing on Saint Ste - phen's Night.
- ing,
dim.
30
mp
mp
mp
mf
34
mp

38
WENCESLAS
mp
mf
WEN.
And this poor man, who was lost in the fo - rest,
S.
A.
p
mp
oo
in the
T.
B.
p
mp
oo
mf
42
mp
Lost in the fo - rest so far a - way.
p
fo - rest
oo
so
p
oo
mp

46
mf
Now be - neath my roof he's smil - ing,
mp
far a - way. My roof, he's smil - -
mp
mf ma dolce
50
smil - ing on Saint Ste - phen's Day.
- ing, smil - ing on Saint Ste - phen's Day.
unis. mf
But
mp

55
S.
A.
mp
in the fo - rest,
T.
B.
all poor souls who must sleep in the fo - rest,
mf
59
sleep all a - lone. To -
sleep in the fo - rest all a - lone.
T.
B.
63
cresc.
- night be - neath his roof, his roof, they're wel - come,
cresc.
cresc.

67
f
wel - come to a home from home, from
f
f
home, from home, from
71
home, from home, home from home,
home, home from home, from
home, home from home,
75
dim.
poco rit.
p dolce
home.
But
home from home.
dim.
p dolce
poco rit.
dim.

79
a tempo
there is a King with a heart so warm. He
a tempo
p dolce
83
melts the ice and calms the storm. He
87
mp
brings us fire and drink and food,
mp
mp

make life good.
91
mf
ev - 'ry - thing to make life, make life good. But
mf
AUDIENCE or SEMI-CHORUS
96
mf
In his mas - ter's steps he trod, Where the snow lay dint - ed;
S.
A.
there is a King with a heart so warm. He
T.
B.
mf

100
Heat was in the ve - ry sod Which the saint had print - ed.
melts the ice and calms the storm. He
104
f
There - fore, ev - 'ry - one, be sure, Wealth or rank pos - sess - ing,
f
brings us fire and drink and food,
f
f

108
Ye who now will bless the poor, Shall your - selves find bless -
ev - 'ry - thing to make, make life
112
poco rit.
a little slower
- ing.
mf ma dolce
good. On Saint Ste - phen's Night our
mf ma dolce
poco rit.
a little slower
mf

Processed in England by Enigma Music Production Services, Amersham, Bucks.
Printed in England by Halstan & Co. Ltd, Amersham, Bucks.